Months of the Year

May

by Robyn Brode

Reading consultant: Susan Nations, M.Ed.,
author/literacy coach/consultant

WEEKLY **WR** READER®
EARLY LEARNING LIBRARY

Please visit our web site at: www.earlyliteracy.cc
For a free color catalog describing Weekly Reader® Early Learning Library's list
of high-quality books, call 1-877-445-5824 (USA) or 1-800-387-3178 (Canada).
Weekly Reader® Early Learning Library's fax: (414) 336-0164.

Library of Congress Cataloging-in-Publication Data

Brode, Robyn.
    May / by Robyn Brode.
      p. cm. — (Months of the year)
    Summary: An introduction to some of the characteristics, events, and activities
of the month of May.
    ISBN 0-8368-3580-8 (lib. bdg.)
    ISBN 0-8368-3616-2 (softcover)
    1. May (Month)—Juvenile literature.   2. Holidays—United States—Juvenile literature.
[1. May (Month).]   I. Title.
GT4803.B7693   2003
394.262—dc21
                                      2002034326

First published in 2003 by
Weekly Reader® Early Learning Library
330 West Olive Street, Suite 100
Milwaukee, WI 53212 USA

Editor: Robyn Brode
Art direction, design, and page production: Leonardo Montenegro with Orange Avenue
Models: Olivia Byers-Strans, Isabella Leary, Madeline Leary
Weekly Reader® Early Learning Library art direction: Tammy Gruenewald
Weekly Reader® Early Learning Library editor: Mark J. Sachner

Photo credits: Cover, p. 7 © Comstock Images; title, pp. 11, 13, 15, 19 © Getty Images;
p. 9 Leonardo Montenegro; pp. 17, 21 © PictureQuest

Printed in the United States of America

1 2 3 4 5 6 7 8 9 07 06 05 04 03

Note to Educators and Parents

Reading is such an exciting adventure for young children! They are beginning to integrate their oral language skills with written language. To help this process along, books must be meaningful, colorful, engaging, and interesting; they should invite young readers to make inquiries about the world around them.

Months of the Year is a new series of books designed to help children learn more about each of the twelve months. In each book, young readers will learn about festivals, celebrations, weather, and other interesting facts about each month.

Each book is specially designed to support the young reader in the reading process. The familiar topics are appealing to young children and invite them to re-read — again and again. The full-color photographs and enhanced text further support the student during the reading process.

These books are designed to be read within an instructional guided reading group. This small group setting allows beginning readers to work with a fluent adult model as they make meaning from the text. After children develop fluency with the text and content, the book can be read independently. Children and adults alike will find these books supportive, engaging, and fun!

— Susan Nations, M.Ed., author, literacy coach, and consultant in literacy development

May is the fifth month of the year. May has 31 days.

May

1	2	3	4	5	6	7
8	9	10	11	12	13	14
15	16	17	18	19	20	21
22	23	24	25	26	27	28
29	30	31				

May is a spring month. In some places, flowers are blooming everywhere.
In May, it is fun to go to the playground or park and play.

May 1 is May Day.
It is a day when some
children like to dance
around a maypole and
play games together.

9

Cinco de Mayo means the Fifth of May in Spanish. On Cinco de Mayo, people celebrate Mexican culture with special foods, music, and dancing.

The second Sunday in May is Mother's Day. Kids give their mothers cards and gifts and tell their mothers how much they love them.

On Mother's Day, kids also give cards to their grandmothers and other women who are special.

Who will you give a card to on Mother's Day?

Memorial Day is at
the end of May. It is a
holiday to remember all
the men and women who
ever lost their lives in war.

In some places, school ends in May. In other places, school ends in June.

When does your school year end?

When May ends,
it is time for June to
begin. Soon it will be
time for summer fun!

Glossary

May Day — the first day of May, when festivals are sometimes held with dancing and games

Memorial Day — a holiday to give thanks to those who died for their country

Mother's Day — a day to thank Mom and other women who are special to us

Months of the Year

1	January	7	July
2	February	8	August
3	March	9	September
4	April	10	October
5	**May**	11	November
6	June	12	December

Seasons of the Year

Winter	Summer
Spring	Fall

About the Author

Robyn Brode wrote the *Going Places* children's book series and was the editor for *Get Out!*, which won the 2002 Disney Award for Hands-On Activities. She has been an editor, writer, and teacher in the book publishing field for many years. She earned a Bachelors in English Literature from the University of California at Berkeley.